EVERYTHING
SEEN AND UNSEEN

GOD IN THE QUANTUM DOMAIN

WRITTEN BY
DERRICK MICHAEL REID

Published by Franklin Publishers
Printed in the United States of America

For permissions, inquiries, or additional copies, contact:
Franklin Publishers
www.franklinpublishers.com

Dedication

This book is dedicated to my stepfather, Hugh Martin Pickens, (DOB 5/28/1938). Hugh stuffed cigarette packs in cigarette machines in Los Angeles County, and in 1960, he married my mother, Edith Ann Woods (DOB 11/17/1930 to 7/14/2023 RIP). Both were raised in Martin's Ferry, Ohio. Mom had five small children from a previous marriage, Gigi 10, David 8, Douglas 7, Derrick 6 and Debra 5. He became a highly skilled machinist, working long hours, while providing for us five siblings with a home and a happy childhood. Hugh proved a stepfather's love for his stepchildren can be boundless and good.

Biography of Derrick Michael Reid BS JD Esq.

Reid graduated from UC Berkeley Engineering with 10 years of design experience working on the first Space Shuttle, the F16, and cruise missile navigation. Reid graduated from WSU Law School and became a patent litigator and prosecutor for 25 years. Reid has 10 years of monetary, 20 years of military, and 20 years of geopolitical self-education. Reid has 3 years of emulator combat experience. Reid ran for the US Presidency in 2016 and the US Senate in 2018. Reid is an engineer, lawyer, systems analyst, monetarist, politician, military scientist, geopolitical analyst, theist, philosopher and Libertarian running for the 2028 US Presidency. Website: DMRCommentary.com FB Group: Libertarian US President 2028.

Prologue

The purpose of this thesis is to provide a translation of the Almighty into the quantum domain so that non-believers, science professionals, and atheistic physicists can comprehend the ubiquitous presence of God, create the most profound work of art in human history for the Glory of God, provide a plot for a documentary depicting the God Hypothesis for triggering a global revival, and, give hope and vision for the future of faith and the world, all through a sublime grand unification, God in the quantum domain.

In January 2021, I started pondering debates between spiritualists and materialists and began intensely studying relevant physics at the quantum and cosmological levels, as well as the relationship between theology and physics. The latter touches upon quantum particles and Big Bang cosmology, the former touching upon free will and miraculous existential explanations, while both touching upon the consciousness and evolution of human beings. I have long studied the sciences and theology, particularly physics, creation and genetics, but became fascinated with the philosophical debates between renowned theologians and physicists.

Main Beach Lifeguard Tower, Laguna Beach, California

Particularly, atheistic physicists and devout theologians have difficulty seeing eye to eye, the former disbelieving in divinity as not being subject to any calculus they understand, the latter recognizing the inabilities of academia to explain why there is existence. These two camps are unable to come together agreeing on a sublime grand unification, because the two perspectives are entrenched in modern bipolar thought of spiritualism and materialism.

My primary studies and thoughts are about the nature of reality and existence. The subsequent revelations were grand and sublime, unifying everything seen and unseen. To most, this sublime grand unification will be skeptically viewed. Unless one has a good understanding of theology, philosophy, physics, genetics and consciousness, it may be difficult to comprehend the true import, for there is nothing grander than revelations of the meaning of life. So, please follow along, for in the end, your understanding and grasping of the concepts presented may provide each of you an increase in the meaning of your own lives and the true theological and physical relationships surrounding us all in the world in which we live.

Spiritualists and Materialists have difficulty understanding everything seen and unseen and perceive the cosmos and the world, that is, heaven and earth, from differing and often conflicting perspectives, particularly related to theology, physics, genetics and mind. The following analysis hopes to unite conflicting perspectives with a common singular understanding of everything seen and unseen. It is encouraged for all to keep an open mind, while traveling through this spiritual and intellectual adventure.

The stage is set for a creative mind to devise a theory of the existence of such a sublime grand unification. The epistemological approach is based on a rational belief that the mind is primary and matter is derivative. The mind can be translated into the quantum domain to provide a scientific ontological explanation of the comprehensive whole. From a detailed analysis of the universe, a work of art will be commissioned to embed this explanation as a tangible expression of everything seen and unseen. This artistic form of expression conveys meaning and comprehension to the viewers. Consequently, I am writing this proposal before submission to the great art galleries of North America and Europe, seeking extensive collaboration enabling the creation of the most profound work of art in human history, appropriately conceived here in Laguna Beach, California and revealed for the first time herein.

Laguna Beach Library, Laguna Beach, California

Everything Seen and Unseen

Driven to comprehend God's Works, that is the material physical world, early Christian thinkers from the Renaissance era pondered and observed the physical universe and developed the Scientific Method. Early Christian Physicists were motivated to understand the surrounding physical world, believing there was an intelligible order created through direct divine involvement, which order was believed to be discoverable. Believing that a divine creative mind was primary and materialism was derivative, they endeavored to understand the mathematical, physical laws of God's Works. Copernicus, Kepler, Galileo, Newton, Maxwell and many other early Christian Physicists led the way to profound scientific revelations and discoveries while cementing the scientific method as the way to comprehend God's Works, the physical realities.

The twentieth century witnessed the rise of atheistic materialism, where matter is primary, and the mind is derivative, providing no explanation for everything in existence, the answers to all pertinent questions. Atheistic materialism had such zeal for proven comprehension that it has led to widely adopted absurdities, such as multiverses or evolution to higher biological morphologies and consciousness through destructive random mutations. This atheism led away from the inexplicable God Hypothesis that is beyond their present intellectual calculus. The combination of materialistic Darwinism and dehumanizing socialism led

4

to the slaughter of 100,000,000 people in the 20th century, for without divine inspiration and gracious individuality, any evil is possible on any macro-scale imaginable.

However, and significantly beyond measure for humanity, with advances in quantum mechanics, intelligent design, information theory, and consciousness enablement, a subtle global revival is underway. This is actually centered in the scientific intelligentsia and profoundly supports, in greater strength, a return of the God Hypothesis. As such, now is the time, the first time in history, for mankind to render the most profound artistic expression possible of the sublime grand unification of God's Word and God's Works, Theology and Physics.

A rational, plausible spiritual quantum field theory of spiriton quantum particles, which interact and are integral with all standard model quantum particles, is proposed, enabling mind over matter, where consciousness is primary and materialism is derivative, supporting the God Hypothesis. Particularly, an infinite number of spiriton quantum particles disposed in a singularity can not only create the universe by thought, that is, by word alone, but also cause any so-called miracle desired by a supreme conscious personal agent. Each of us, made in the image of God, possess spiriton quantum particles in our brains, giving rise to an individual consciousness as a free will personal agency. Spiriton quantum particles are massless bosons bounded and integrated for forming a mind and spirit of free will. Under this theory of everything seen and unseen, a divine conscious singularity can sense and know everything and perfect any changes desired in all quantum fields. The divine can change any quantum particle instantaneously anywhere in the cosmos, comprising heaven and earth, reaching out through entangled spooky actions, and thus, the means to manage, alter and control everything, such as creation, life and evolution, among all things.

Present-day physical understandings, though making fantastic discoveries over the last few centuries, are nothing more than the realization of mathematical formulae describing how matter, energy and space-time work, and do so with phenomenal accuracies. But describing how something works or behaves or its quantification is not a description or understanding of what that something is. Every bit of matter and energy can be reduced to quantum particles consisting of fermions of mass and bosons of force, which are effectively the same thing because E=m(c-squared). That's it. There is a great discovery among many that has remained elusive in the physics discipline. The extraordinarily weak and hence the undetectable graviton enables gravity and the warping of space-time, the last bit of discovery necessary for a physical grand unification of the description of all known quantum particles and effects by a singular mathematical expression. The graviton enabling gravity and the spiriton enabling consciousness have remained elusive to scientific experimental detection, characterization, and quantification.

Each quantum particle is a fluctuating probabilistic wave function of mathematical perturbations transiting quantum fields, which are quantum spatial constructs. Thus, reality is no more than mathematical fluctuations in spatial constructs. Thus, nothing is real, but all is an illusion based on mathematical expressions and constructs, a matrix, giving rise to information theories of universal simulations and cosmic holograms. All quantum particles can be described by and are essentially information, a non-tangible illusory realization of everything.

When one sees a perceived physical object, it is the brain recording an image of an arrangement of received photons. That is, one does not see an object directly, but rather records a photonics arrangement, pixilated information, which is nothing more than a form of photography. There is no difference between seeing an image and seeing a photograph. Photonic perception is an illusion, for one can never see the actual thing but only a photonic image of the thing imaged. When one feels a perceived physical object, it is the outer electrons exchanging virtual photons that give rise to electrostatic repulsion forces that are actually felt. But at no time is there actual contact to be sensed. Quantum particles give rise to the sensation of touch, but there is no touching at all. The sense of touch is also an illusion of reality.

The physical universe, made exclusively of quantum particles, does not create anything new but can form new bodies from preexisting material. Gravity may force together matter to where fusion ignites a new star, but gravity did not create the star but merely formed a new star from preexisting matter. The physics of gravity pressure causing high temperature causing fusion was not created, only the forming of a new star was realized under conservation of energy. Mathematical physical laws do not create new matter or energy but may cause the rearrangement of existing material and energy into new forms, such as combining hydrogen and oxygen into water, an atomic transformation into a molecular reality.

The same can be said for quantum foam, where matter and antimatter particles originate from space-time and energy levels within quantum fields, which is not nothing, which is not a void, which is something, and this something is being transformed into the opposing particles formed and annihilated, from zero energy back to zero energy, within mathematical laws of physics. Quantum foam is not a creation but merely another form of transformation within mathematical physical laws. However, when a universe is created out of a void, out of nothing, that creation requires an infinite conscious mind, an all-powerful personal agency, God Almighty.

Lutheran Church of the Cross, Woodland Hills, California

Physical matter does not create mathematical laws of physics but merely obeys mathematical laws of physics. Fusion does not create new atoms, nor does a supernova create new atoms, but rather fusion and supernova form new atoms according to preexisting mathematical laws of physics using preexisting matter. Fusion and supernovas do not reorder the quantum mechanical states of electrons, which all gold atoms have. Nothing novel was created. The formed gold atoms are not novel, being the same old gold atoms long made by exploding stars using existing matter, the transformation being by a fused combination of light chemical elements into heavy chemical elements. Parents do not create babies, but rather they form babies transformed from preexisting DNA and preexisting nutrients.

The creation of something new that is different in kind and not derived exclusively from preexisting matter and energy requires the employment of creativity, which only comes from the mind. Creation can only come from the mind. DNA, for example, is a literary work, a special kind of writing, a computer code, which can not be formed by only physical laws and the transformation of preexisting matter, but requires creativity as all writings do.

Mathematics is also a language of writing, having grammar and syntax. Mathematical laws can not be formed by preexisting matter. Mathematical laws must be created by an intelligent mind. The cosmological constants, which are precise to one part in ten thousand trillion trillion trillion trillion, to enable life, cannot be formed by preexisting matter and mathematical laws. Mathematical laws and their constants must be created. The creation of the mathematical laws of physics requires a creative mind. Whether it be literary writings, computer codes, or mathematical laws, the writings are organized information with grammar and syntax written for particular purposes and functions, and these writings cannot be formed by random processes or by matter, but only created by a creative mind.

Structured writings require intelligent design. Regardless of the medium in which the writings are embedded, all writings are creative, and intelligence is required to organize symbolic constituents of a language into meaningful messages, be it a literary work, a computer code, or a mathematical expression. Intelligent design requires an intelligent mind, which must precede matter, energy, and life with descriptions to enable a physical realization and manifestations in the first instance. Cosmology and life are the two great mysteries that comprise the most sublime question of all, why does anything exist? Life is a perplexing phenomenon. It seems clear from the geological and paleontological records of 5 billion years that some form of evolution has occurred, first referenced by theologians thousands of years ago in the Genesis creation story.

There are five main arguments against Darwinism, the theory of evolution by natural selection in gradual mutations, consisting of the difficulty explaining the origin of complex structures, the lack of clear transitional fossils, the problem of explaining the sudden appearance of species in the fossil record; the failure to definitively map a "tree of life" using molecular biology; and the challenge of explaining convergent evolution. Darwinism struggles to explain the origin of complex and intricate structures and systems, like the eye, where the development of all parts is necessary for function, known as irreducible complexity. While the fossil record offers evidence of past life, clear transitional forms between major groups of organisms are often lacking, making it difficult to visualize gradual evolution. The fossil record shows the abrupt appearance of many species without clear ancestors, which contradicts the gradualistic nature of Darwinian theory. Despite advances in molecular biology, a definitive "tree of life" based on common ancestry has been difficult to construct, raising questions about the universality of the theory. The phenomenon where unrelated species independently evolve similar traits, like the eyes of squids and mammals, challenges the idea that all life is descended from a common ancestor.

Darwinism cannot explain creation, such as the beginning of life, or rapid morphological diversity, such as the Cambrian Explosion. Darwinism has a fatal flaw, now recognized, that random destructive physical mutation processes can not create differing improved morphologies but only degrade existing functional morphologies. Try randomly flipping bits of a computer operating system code and watch how fast the system crashes. Darwinism, at best, explains biological adaptations enabled by preexisting DNA within the preexisting morphologies of species, such as differently shaped finch beaks, such as individual features of eye color, hair color, size, and so on. Adaptions do not reach the level of new morphologies. Adaptations are not morphological changes. Adaptations can evolve through three types of control functions such as by unnatural selection through selective breeding, natural selection through preferences, or by random selection through happenstance. These three types of procreation by coupling parents transform existing DNA by combining preexisting DNA.

DNA transformations allow for species adaptations confine to respective morphologies. The DNA transformation of existing species with existing morphologies into new species with new morphologies occurs by intelligent design, the creative mind generating the preexisting DNA having coded routines for forming new species with new body plans of changed morphologies through designed DNA alterations. Darwin got it partially correct that the selection process can cause adaptations but got it wrong, suggesting random mutations were the source of morphological change. Rather, transformations of the DNA are not mutations but preplanned or pre-enabled evolution of the code derived from the initial creation of the code or from divine intervention altering the DNA code, but in either case, it requires intelligent design by a creative mind.

The DNA code, as intelligently designed, allows for adaptations less we all be identical clones. Selective breeding, natural selection and random selection do not cause random mutations but can adaptively form enhanced features and adaptations using preexisting DNA while transforming the DNA over time, and thus, the DNA computer code goes through changes with resulting adaptation changes. Extreme adaptations do not reach the level of new morphologies and new species. Hence, biological evolution, which requires an enabling DNA code requiring intelligent design or a miraculous rewriting of the DNA code, also requires intelligent design. In either case of embedded enablement or miraculous recoding, evolution requires intelligent design requiring an intelligent mind.

It is thus plausible that Homoerectus evolved into Homosapians, Neanderthals, and Denisons using embedded DNA code transforming itself over long time periods, allowing for adaptations and species differentiation as a consequence of the original DNA sequence. It is equally plausible that an intelligent designer created a superior human consciousness by a miraculous intervention. Darwinism can't explain irreducible biological complexity that precludes a gradual evolution over time. Paleontologists have discovered stepped and explosive evolutionary morphological changes precluding a gradual change in morphologies. Darwinism is dead, and another explanation of morphological change is now indispensable.

Big Bang cosmology, the theological beginning, morphological evolution, and the theological Genesis are very clear examples of where the theologians got it right thousands of years ago. Although academia has made fantastic gains in understanding the mathematical and physical order, there is much more to be discovered, with academia finally starting to catch up to what theologians knew long ago. The Big Bang and Genesis are the most profound creation events from a personal God, deciding when to create heavens and earth 13.8 billion years ago with cosmological constants enabling life such that God and mankind could have a personal relationship that is good.

The divine cause of the universe inevitably must be timeless, for time was only then created; spaceless for space was only then created; immaterial for matter was only then created, all-powerful as the universe is colossal, all-knowing and intelligently creative as the life enabling cosmological constants are finely tuned with exquisite precision, and personal in temporally creating the means for fellowship with mankind. God is eternal, the alpha and the omega, an uncaused cause that is timeless, spaceless, immaterial, all-powerful, all-knowing, personal and good.

Physicists do not address creation or creativity but rather only discover the mathematical ordering of the physical world. Physicists only discover physical, mathematical laws. For example, physicists have discovered that $F=ma$, that force equals mass multiplied by acceleration, but not why it is so or how that relationship was created. Physicists cannot tell you the creative WHY, but only the mathematical HOW, by repeating empirical confirming experiments generating experimental data. Theologians may be able to adopt the explanations of HOW by scientific interpretations of God's Works, but importantly can explain the WHY by interpreting spiritual minds. The two disciplines, Theology and Physics, while modernly disjointed in causal discovery and interpretive means, have traditionally been combined by early Christian physicists. Newton, who marveled at how God maintained the planets in orbit, determined the mathematical law of gravity. Newton got it right that gravity was created, not formed.

Saint Mary's Episcopal Church, Laguna Beach, California

The purpose of the Scientific Method as applied to physics is to discover ultimately the mathematical laws of nature. By this very purpose and means, physics is limited to the discoveries of repeated verifiable mathematical laws that describe recurrent physical phenomena. While the discipline of physics and the means of the scientific method have made great advances in understanding the physical universe, they can not explain non-recurrent meta-physical phenomena such as The Big Bang, the creation of life, miracles, the resurrection and ascension, consciousness, literary creation, evolution of coded DNA, artistic creation, subjective experiences, informational quantum particles and fields, and ultimately the creation of information. Physics and the scientific method do not and cannot address the mind and information by a recurrent calculus, despite grandiose proclamations to the contrary.

A glaring example of scientific pretension is the multiverse postulation for explaining the anthropic principle of fine-tuning, where spiritually limited scientific minds attempt to explain why the universe is finely tuned to support life through an infinite number of multiverses. No direct answer is known as to why the universe is finely tuned to support life, and so the scientific community must make up an answer without a scientific foundation to avoid the theological best explanation. So adverse is the scientific academia to mathematical modeling of a creator, mind, consciousness and intelligent design within the comprehensive whole explanation of the universe, that absurd theories are tabled in a desperate attempt to avoid integrating mind, consciousness and ultimately theology into the quantum domain as the best explanation.

The self-centered grandiose pretensions are obvious when absurd theories are proposed that can never be tested for verification within the scientific method, the means science employs to discover. These scientific pretensions discard the scientific method so as to propose theories that discount the mind as the best explanation for fine-tuning because the mind currently is not quantified within the quantum domain, and thus does not fit within the limited understanding of scientific academia, and thus such frivolous and made up theories are inherently suspect, as well as lacking serious foundation and credibility necessary for consideration.

It is conscious awareness that collapses the quantum wave function into a deterministic particle, as in monitoring quantum particles transitioning in the well-known double slit experiment, showing that a quantum particle can be detected as a wave function or as a particle function. Thus, consciousness is fundamental and bounded in the brain or out of the body and must be interactive at the quantum level. Yet, despite the well-known fundamental interaction of the mind in the quantum domain, many physicists refuse to incorporate the mind into the standard model, for once the mind is translated into the quantum domain, an extrapolation to an all-powerful deity becomes feasible. This is like the resistance to believe the universe had a beginning, which necessarily gives rise to an all powerful creator, from overwhelming circumstantial evidence, exercising a personal free will decision to create the cosmos. This is similar to the unfounded belief that life spawned from a primordial soup through random molecular occurrences, which is mathematically impossible. The scientific community desperately holds on to limited and inadequate explanations of reality to avoid the inclusion of mind and creation into the calculus of physical reality based upon supreme notions of materialism cemented by self-centered scientific pretensions.

Those physicists who overreach their discipline through scientific pretenses, use mathematical laws of physics to present nothing proven by the scientific method, to form unfounded beliefs in creation based solely on those mathematical laws, and thereby confuse the difference between divine creation and mathematical formulation. Hawking's declaration that a gravity law can create a universe is an example of philosophical absurdities that physicists will attempt to use in physics to glorify themselves as the most important of all. Only a mind can create, and the mathematical laws of physics can only be used to transform matter and energy, which cannot create anything. The admitted inability by atheistic physicists to even postulate what a quantum particle actually is underscores their inherent inability to place mind over matter in the quantum domain.

The two means of deriving something new, creation and transformation, are not mutually exclusive, though, for the mind can not only create but can also transform, if powerful enough, the mind being primary and matter being derivative. Miracles are defined as a created transformation outside the normal unguided transformation processes obeying only physical mathematical laws. When a mind transforms physical matter outside the mathematical, physical laws, it is an act of creation by a creative mind, commonly known as a miracle, by those lacking an understanding of the comprehensive whole, comprising the translation of the mind into the quantum domain.

Atheistic physicists reject miracles that are creative transformations as inconsistent with the mathematical laws of physics. They have discovered over the centuries that scientific pretensions for physics are a limited discipline directed to the discovery of the observable mathematical order, and not the creative mind yet. But a fundamental change is occurring right now, in the 21st century, where neuroscience is being directed to understanding the quantum nature of consciousness and the necessary platform of the human creative brain. Mankind is on the threshold of understanding quantum particle arrangements, producing consciousness as a creative mind. When the human mind is translated into the quantum domain, the human mind could then be extrapolated to an infinite mind of the Almighty. In the far future, it could very well be that super artificial intelligence becomes conscious through quantum computing and spiriton emulation.

An infinite mind existed at the time of universal creation and disposed in an infinitesimal singularity within a Planck volume, the smallest cubic volume possible, though the Planck volume is infinitely large compared to a singularity. The initial quantum fluctuations of the Big Bang were caused by an infinite arrangement of spiriton quantum particles as a divine creative mind disposed in an infinitesimally small singularity, thereby translating the Almighty into the quantum domain in the universe for the first time. The mind, be it divinely infinite or humanly minute, is the source of creativity and creation. The infinite mind created the mathematical order discoverable by scientific minds. Physicists actually only possess scientific data sufficient for formulating mathematical laws through empirical experimental data.

The mathematical order allows for the transformation of matter and energy within universal symmetries as a conservation of energy and momentum. When the infinite mind transforms matter and energy outside the mathematical order, it is referred to as a miracle by limited minds. When a mind creates writing containing only information, it is an act of creativity. When minute minds transform matter and energy through experiments within the mathematical order, it is creativity. The majority of physicists limit their view of reality to their discipline of only the discovery of the mathematical order and no more. Instances of creation and creativity are outside their focus, and their scientific methods cannot reach the calculus of creation and creativity yet.

Psychologists are focused on characterizing consciousness and determining how consciousness works, but not the necessary quantum arrangement giving rise to mind. However, neuroscience is beginning to address the physical formation of matter supporting consciousness and the resulting mind, and from that, develop an understanding and description of the quantum arrangement of coded information, giving rise to consciousness, thus describing the formation of mind and resulting creativity, from its DNA source, which is further information. In the centuries to come, mankind will marvel, by extrapolation, at the mind of the all-knowing and all-powerful Almighty.

Saddleback Church Lake Forest, California

Humans are made in the image of God, and that means free will, personal agency, being God-like, though of limited creative power inherent in the minute human conscious mind. The quantum mechanical nature of the human mind, however, can be extrapolated to infinity to encompass a realization of the Almighty. The probabilistic nature of a quantum wave function is analogous to a conscious mind weighing decisions, and thus, it is natural for a conscious mind to be formed from illusory information described by writing the DNA code. Thus, consciousness is created in the quantum domain as an image of God.

God created man in his image on Earth by intelligent design by writing DNA codes in evolutionary steps for creating physical brains having bounded spiritons for creating human consciousness, the mind being in God's image. Consciousness is a state of awareness of oneself and one's surroundings. It encompasses mental processes, including thoughts, feelings, perceptions, and awareness of one's own existence. Consciousness is a subjective experience of the world and oneself. The only reality that is absolute is our own consciousness and our own existence, for forming a loving praising communion with God Almighty, giving man potential for peace on earth and in our hearts, and giving mankind the gift of eternal joy and salvation in communion with God, an eternal, uncaused cause, the alpha and the omega, the supreme ruler of the universe.

Once the hard problem of consciousness is solved, explaining consciousness from the brain neuro-mass, extrapolated to divinity, can be realized, at which point theology becomes understandable by atheistic physicists as being explained in physical terms. The hard problem is solved by a bounded integrated positive feedback collection of spiriton quantum particles forming human consciousness localized in the brain. Thus, the fundamental nature of mankind is that consciousness is emergent from the brain. Eastern religions are flawed because, in all cases, people are collectively joined by thought, when humans are actually individuals of separate free wills, disjointed and separated, requiring individual salvation. The only sure aspect of reality is individual consciousness that is divorced from a divine entity in the material world, "I think, therefore I am," and not also someone else. In all cases, consciousness is localized to an individual physical brain, a homogeneous one-to-one and onto mapping, between individual brains and respective individual consciousness with transient out-of-body experiences, such as awareness by the collapsing quantum wave function. A bounded integrated cloud of fundamental spiriton quantum particles can exist out of the body as ghosts indefinitely as an individual soul, but lacking physical means for communications with living persons.

The hard problem of mind and consciousness is the explanation of thought and subjective experiences from physical brain neuro-systems, the only materialistic explanation. Correlations are found between brain locations and subjective experiences. The easy problem of mind and consciousness is explaining behavior through behavior psychology. There currently is no materialistic explanation for the mind and consciousness from the physical brain, and yet the mind is the creative source of information that characterizes the entire physical universe. There is no materialistic explanation for the creation of life, morphological evolution, creation of the universe, and informational quantum particles. There is circumstantial evidence and explanations for creation through the mind, a personal agency.

Thus, the stage is set for a description of everything seen and unseen, where consciousness is the key to mind to bring God's Word and God's Work together as a sublime grand unification, for the first time in human history. Materialism can not explain existence, creation, morphological evolution, or consciousness, as well as dark energy, dark matter, on the cosmic scale, or three phase states of fermions, or the illusive gravitons, or even what is energy or a quantum particle. While the scientific method has provided profound discoveries, in the comprehensive view, science is still in its infancy.

Spiritualism from bounded integrated spiriton minds can explain many things, such as universal creation, consciousness and life creation based upon direct and circumstantial evidence. This can also explain quantum particles and morphological evolution based on creative writings from a creative mind. Also included are miraculous transformations based upon a creative mind, where direct historical evidence and declaratory evidence, such as the excited utterances during the ascension, the life of God incarnate, and resurrection of God on earth, and the sustained conspiratorial lives, ministries and willing deaths of the apostles. These circumstantial and direct proofs of divinity, while acceptable proofs in a court of civil law, are, however, unacceptable to atheistic physicists who limit their inquiry only to the scientific method, which had its roots in the discovery of God's works and not God's word.

The creation of the cosmos, the creation of life, the morphological evolution, the resurrection, and the ascension are, by their very nature, one-off events that do not fit within the scientific method of repeatability. The many singular proofs abundantly supporting the God Hypothesis are outside the narrow and limited scientific method. While the scientific method has produced profound discoveries of God's works, it is unsuited for determining the existence of mind and divinity. For example, Scientists should not speak to the state of consciousness when they have absolutely no credible understanding of how the mind has subjective experiences from brain neuro-mass. Nevertheless, under limitations of the scientific method, atheistic physicists under scientific pretensions will proclaim absurdities outside the scope of their science and scientific method and boldly enter the philosophical, theological and cognitive disciplines with unsubstantiated unproven proclamations that are unavoidably and conspicuously suspect.

From the totality of circumstances and discoveries, an agency-conscious spiriton quantum particle and an agency-conscious spiriton quantum field are proposed as a final necessary element for explaining everything seen and unseen. The agency quantum spiriton particles are fundamental and interact with themselves in the agency spiriton quantum field for forming consciousness of a mind. These agency-conscious spiriton quantum particles can be localized to physical brains for earthly

21

creatures, including man, and localized in the cosmos for heavenly spirits when eternally disposed. These conscious spiriton quantum particles and the conscious spiriton quantum field interact with other quantum particles and quantum fields for forming knowledge, intelligence, and relationships, and interact with themselves for forming consciousness, thought, mind, creativity and free will, and thus, a theory of everything as the most plausible explanation. The fundamental consciousness is reduced to the quantum level and though outside of traditional physics of physical reality, is nonetheless an inescapable part of the comprehensive whole. This will be adopted as fundamental by the scientific academia when both correlated brain function and conscious experiences unite as repeated measured occurrences of mind activity.

The graviton bosons and spiriton bosons quantum particles await discovery in the centuries to come. Quantum gravity and consciousness are two major areas in need of scientific explanation. The graviton boson is an undetected force particle, a fundamental quantum particle that warps space-time when interacting with fermions, which are mass quantum particles, quarks and leptons, for forming gravity in space-time. A spiriton boson is an undetected force particle, a fundamental quantum particle that forms bounded integrated minds of experiences with decisive collapsing wave functions, which are probabilistic positions of quantum particles, fermions and bosons, for forming consciousness in space-time. These two gravity and consciousness fundamental particles are apparent from reality, as the earth revolves around the sun and as, "I think, therefore I am", respectively.

Thus, everything is reduced to quantum particles in quantum fields, enabling both matter and mind, and thereby explaining everything seen and unseen. An infinite group of spiriton quantum particles enables divine interaction with all quantum particles and thus an ability to perfect miracles at will on any scale imaginable. This is the most plausible trajectory of scientific inquiry in the centuries to come, the direct scientific discovery of God, finally catching up to theology. In the millennia to come, super artificial intelligence may become conscious through quantum computing and spiriton emulation.

There is no possible way to extrapolate in time before the Big Bang or time within the first Planck period, and thus, the extrapolation from human consciousness to divine consciousness is limited to our temporal current epoch understanding of the universe. But within the universal knowledge as currently understood, a new theory of everything is now possible and can be articulated with rational plausibility. This rational plausibility shall be reduced to an artistic form of expression, a work of art entitled *Everything Seen and Unseen*.

St. James Episcopal Church, Newport Beach,
California, Baptized 1981

In a concise statement of everything, physics, theology, genetics and consciousness are unified into one theory. Such is the work of art that imparts to its viewers a profound understanding of everything. The physical world, materialism, does indeed reduce all things, not to just repeatable macro material physical realities, but to fluctuating information of quantum particles, that are fundamental informational manipulating quantum particles, transiting information constructs, that are quantum fields. Consciousness is the ability of information of spiriton quantum particles to manipulate information to create new information in spiriton quantum particles, and thus, consciousness and spiriton quantum information are also fundamental, reduced to the quantum domain. Gluons create chromodynamics of three quarks to bind them within protons and neutrons. Similarly, spiritons can be bonded in a

24

cloud of spiritons, and integrated in such a way as to provide interaction for forming the mind, the image of god, and move within quantum fields throughout the universe as an eternal spirit.

There are the bosons consisting of the spiriton, gluon, W/Z, photon, graviton and Higgs bosons, which are force quantum particles, and also there are the fermions mass quantum particles consisting of quarks which are the up quarks and down quarks, and of leptons which are the neutrinos and electrons. At time zero, within a void, there existed an infinite stack of spiritual force spiriton bosons, God in the quantum domain. A finite number of the infinity of spiritual force spiritons bosons, in a sublime grand unification, decay into gravity force graviton bosons, the Higgs bosons, and the grand unification of the strong electromagnetic force bosons, all decaying within the Plank era of a trillionth of a trillionth of a trillionth of a second, the first undecillionth of a second, occurring within the space of a millionth of a millionth of the volume of a quark, of the nascent universe.

During the grand unification epoch, ten million times longer than the Plank era, of ten-thousandths of a trillionth of a trillionth of a trillionth of a trillionth of a second, the strong electromagnetic force bosons then decayed into the strong nuclear force gluon bosons and the weak electromagnetic force bosons, which then decayed into the weak nuclear force W/Z bosons and the electromagnetic force photon bosons, in a volume smaller than a quark quantum particle at a temperature of a hundred thousand trillion trillion degrees Kelvin dropping to a trillion trillion degrees Kelvin energy levels, a trillion times higher than the Cern Hadron Collider. A collider having a diameter greater than the solar system would be required to reach detection energies of the graviton before the grand unification epoch. The detection of the spiriton quantum particle may require a hadron collider the size of the Milky Way, God keeping the mystery in place, allowing mankind free will.

During the grand unification epoch, the strong force breaks free and then the weak force breaks free from the grand unification, as photons decay into fermions including matter and antimatter particle pairs of quarks and leptons, for example, the electron and positron, spontaneously forming and annihilating, back into photons, but due to a slight imbalance there between, antimatter particles were nearly all annihilated, leaving a universe of nearly all matter fermion quantum particles, of the standard model of particle physics.

During this time, the universe then bangs by rapid expansion in an inflationary epoch from the size of a quark of a trillionth of a trillionth of a meter, which is a thousand times smaller than a proton, to eventually reach one hundred million light-years in diameter in less than a second, as the universe cools from a trillion trillion degrees Kelvin to three degrees Kelvin, during which cooling and expansion, is a dark epoch of bounded photons. The photons were then released as the universe expanded and cooled, as in "Let There Be Light" (the motto of my Alma Matar, the University of California), generating the cosmic microwave background as quarks formed neutrons and protons, forming atomic nuclei, as electrons bonded to atomic nuclei, forming atoms, as gravity began to concentrate atoms into dust and early planets, stars, and solar systems, then forming galaxies and quasars with centered black holes, the visible universe as we see it now realized. In a personal agency, God created something from nothing 13.8 billion years ago in a Big Bang, as described in the Genesis Story, creating man by his word for personal communion and loving fellowship on Earth orbiting about a five billion-year-old star, the Sun, in a universe, in a galaxy, the Milky Way, in a solar system, on the planet Earth, subject to God's finely tuned physical laws and creation works, finely tuned to support life and mankind, God being infinitely good, wonderful and sublime.

The Cosmic Microwave Background, "Let There be Light".

The cosmic microwave background is a faint photonic microwave afterglow that fills the sky in every direction of the first light that could travel freely at the start of the dark epoch when the universe became transparent to photons four hundred thousand years after the Big Bang. The cosmic microwave background is nearly uniform and exhibits small temperature fluctuations, one part in one hundred thousand, leading to uniform distribution of planets, stars and galaxies, yet allowing through gravity mass concentrations into those cosmic bodies. This uniformity supports the Big Bang theory that the universe was once hot and dense and has since cooled and expanded as the first observational evidence for the Big Bang theory. This threw atheistic physicists into consternation as it is direct evidence that the universe was created from nothing, supporting the biblical Genesis creation story, when in the beginning, God said by the word, "Let there be light," that in the beginning there was the dark void. The expansion of the universe during the inflationary epoch, from the size of a quark that is one trillionth of a trillionth of a meter to the size of a proton that is a thousandth of a trillionth of a meter, a billionfold increase, in a trillionth of a trillionth of a second, is a miraculous one-off event of creation that even atheistic physicists now believe, as well as expanding a million trillion trillion trillion trillion trillion trillionfold in a thousandth of a second. The nascent expansion and cooling of the universe is a miracle that only the eternal, uncaused cause could cause in preparing a home for mankind to enjoy ever-lasting, peaceful, loving communion with God.

Functional integration of spiritons forming mind, decisions based upon quantum computing and collapsing probabilistic wave functions for thought can have an intermediate origin from biology. DNA, a coded operating system, necessarily created by mind, as all writings are, allows for the formation of the minds in brains. The DNA code forms spiriton microscopic structures within the brain, the structure integrated, for producing thought and consciousness. The microscopic structure can be transformed into existence from a coded DNA writing at the quantum level, enabling thought. Thus, microscopic spiriton structures are nested within DNA, as the intermediate biological origin of the mind in the brain, integrated and bonded. Natural death and biological molecular decay do not destroy the bonded integrated spiriton structure that, now untethered to biological molecular structures, can exist out of the body as an eternal spirit in the quantum domain. Thus, the sublime gray unification of theology and physics is where everything is reduced to informational fundamentals. All things, body and soul, the physical universe, and God are reduced to information in our universe with all of the same intrinsic fundamental nature. The brain is able to physically form micro-structures for containing information manipulating spiriton quantum particles for creating localized individual minds. Heaven is a universal superimposed collection of quantum fields in which information manipulating quantum fluctuations reside, that is, where God, lesser angelic and demonic information-manipulating groupings, and individual souls can reside as free-floating cosmic spirits.

In the beginning of the current universal epoch, at time zero, God existed as an infinite informational quantum stack of spiriton bosons in a sublime grand unification, then decaying by releasing Higgs and graviton bosons into the grand unification of photons, gluons, and W/Z bosons, all superimposed and disposed in a singularity, the spiriton quantum stack of God being timeless, spaceless, immaterial, all powerful, all

28

knowing, and personal, creating the universe from nothing, employing a Big Bang. The mass particles spawn form decaying superimposed photon bosons. The collection of superimposed bosons separated in stages as the universe cooled, from the sublime grand unification, to the electromagnetic strong force and the electromagnetic weak force, into the separated spiriton, Higgs, strong gluon, weak W/Z and photon bosons. The photon stack then decayed into fermion quarks for forming protons and neutrons, and leptons consisting of electrons and neutrinos for forming atoms after the start of the Plank era, to inflationary fine-tuning on a colossal scale. Eventually, this created the universe and life through DNA writings of information, which is intelligent design, with follow-on guided rewriting of DNA writings during the evolutionary epoch. This created and enabled lesser informational manipulating quantum minds, by integrated information theory, for combining consciousness spiriton quantum particles into minds made in God's image, which is in the spiriton quantum particle and quantum field domain in which all minds reside.

Being pervasive throughout the universe, as a fundamental consciousness, and all-powerful, God revealed himself to earthly souls through the resurrection, which is not a metaphysical miracle but the mere quantum-level manipulation of information, a new writing, as all informational writings require a creative mind. String theory and multiverses are excluded from consideration as being outside of science, as with extrapolation before the Big Bang. String theory is a reduction of the standard model to resonant transformations that add nothing to provable science to determining the nature of reality. Theoretical physicists need to acknowledge that there are only 4 dimensions. String theory can not be demonstrated with any credibility. Mathematical constructs to ten dimensions are inconsistent with centuries of highly successful four-dimensional space-time physics and provable discoveries and cannot be seriously considered as a reflection of reality. There is absolutely no experimental data supporting string theory or multiverses, as both are merely mathematical constructs by theoretical physicists desperately attempting to avoid the God Hypothesis. Until there is more than mere hypothetical mathematical formulations, string theory and multiverses are wholly illusory, discredited, unproven and outside centuries of four-dimensional space-time discoveries. Any attempt to minimize the anthropic principle of divine cosmic fine-tuning for supporting human life should be realized for the hollowness that it is. The only plausible explanation for there to be something rather than nothing is a divine creator. Even abstract mathematical constructs cannot exist without the mind.

The characteristics of the conscious spiriton quantum particles would include an ability to collapse quantum particle wave functions for perception, an ability to be combined under integrated information theory, include an ability to be bounded in space-time for localized minds, an include a form of positive feedback for amplified consciousness into new information and thought for creativity. The conscious spiriton quantum particles, like all other quantum particles, consist of information, and in that sense, panpsychism is realized throughout the universe. God exists in our universe as an infinite stack of conscious spiriton quantum particles able to know and manipulate all things and realities. Angelic and demonic entities and lesser souls similarly exist but at lesser degrees, all of whom reside in heaven and hell, which are portions of the cosmic superposition quantum fields. God in our universe took the form of information from which all were created, including mankind, with whom God can have a personal relationship between and among conscious minds.

Ever since the dawn of mankind, some say approximately 200,000 years ago, the first feeble forms of primitive artistic expressions radiated from simple terrestrial minds. An ultimate artistic work has been sought but, to date, has never been conceived or expressed in a tangible form. This artwork will be unique, profound, and priceless, being the first in history to reveal everything that combines theism, quantum theory, gravity, and consciousness in a single work of art, thereby obtaining worldwide recognition. Therefore, an artistic masterpiece is proposed, entitled *Everything Seen and Unseen*. This will place theism into the quantum domain as the only known depiction of a singularly comprehensive explanation of everything, the sublime grand unification. The art expression of everything seen and unseen will rival the great artistic works of the Renaissance. With recent advances in science and philosophy, now is the time for such a rendering.

In one artwork, a comprehensive theory of everything seen and unseen is revealed, minimally including the Theistic Creed, Theistic Trinity, Devine Agency, Quantum Mechanics, Quantum Fields, Spatial Heaven, Angelic and Demonic Populations, Quantum Theory of Everything, Quantum Forces Grand Unification, and Quantum Consciousness. All works mentioned, and more will be depicted in such a way as to join once and for all time, God's Word and God's Works, Theology and Physics, as a profound singular artistic expression of everything seen and unseen portraying the sublime grand unification.

The reduction of all to the informational quantum domain is the sublime grand unification of all and, thus, the theory of everything seen and unseen, the combination of theology, physics, genetics and consciousness, explaining everything seen and unseen. The prospective work of art entitled *Everything Seen and Unseen* is conceptually directed to theology, physics and the interconnected consciousness and genetics of mankind. Thus, conceptually, theology, physics, consciousness and biology will embrace all that is known and seamlessly integrated into a single work of art. A work of art is proposed which includes a first theological portion understood and recognized by study by theologians, a second physical portion understood and recognized by study by physicists, and a third joined portion that draws theologians and physicists to a common understanding of everything seen and unseen, the three portions seamlessly integrated into a comprehensive whole, as a singular work for providing any viewer a profound understanding of everything, and thus, a proposal for a work of art depicting everything seen and unseen.

Though a mental concept only at this time, the work of art comprises a cosmic plane, a quantum field lattice, and a tablet legend. The plane reveals the cosmic microwave background map at its core and extends into quasars, black holes, galaxies and, ultimately, a surrounding holographic representation of the cosmos. Perpendicular to the cosmic microwave background is a super positioned quantum field lattice in which is depicted all forms of realizations. The realizations depict all quantum forms, including mind, forces and matter. The realizations include theological and physical representations readily recognized by theologians and physicists, respectively, but further include realizations that bring together theology and physics in a sublime grand unification. Below the plane and lattice structures is a legend of tablets providing textual information to the viewer so as to impart meaning and understanding of everything seen and unseen through study of the work of art as a whole. After study, the viewer is left with a profound understanding of the universe in which we all live, as the most profound work of art in human history. The actual design, though, currently represents trade secret information. The design will no doubt go through iterations during the design and fabrication process, but some marvelous visions of it have been pictured in mind, including the cosmic plane, quantum field lattice and tabulated legend that give the viewer a profound understanding of everything of the sublime grand unification.

The work of art has an oval cosmic microwave background, around which are galaxies, around which are distal quasars, and around which are binary 0-1 digital information, forming an oval planar depiction of the cosmos. Extended orthogonally are rods depicting quantum fields, attached to which are symbols representing theological and physical concepts. The oval background is disposed in and supported by a dome-shaped oval stand, onto which is a legend of tiles, each of which has a symbol and name, referencing the symbols disposed in the quantum field. For example, a God symbol may be a triangle with infinity, alpha and omega, and sun, cross, and flame disposed in the triangle. A theologian would recognize the god symbol and physicists would recognize quantum particles and quantum field symbols, bringing the two together in a common understanding of everything seen and unseen. An artistic and financial collaboration will be necessary because this work of art will be costly and developed over several years. Once completed, major art galleries and places of worship will clamor to display it in perpetuity for the Glory of God. The title comes from the Nicene Creed.

A documentary premise to be filmed is profound. Characters include: John Lennox, Christopher Hitchens, David Berlinski, Susan Greenfield, David Chalmers, Michael Behe, Roger Penrose, Richard Dawkins, Stephen Hawking, William Craig, Sam Harris, Joe Rogan, Stephen Meyers, and James Tour. Plot: Neuro-micro-structures are discovered containing spiriton quantum particles that are bounded and integrated for forming human consciousness extrapolated to an infinite divinity, converting atheistic physicists into devout Christians in a global revival of the God Hypothesis. The opening, Cern Switzerland Hadron Collider, 2030 graviton discovered, Nobel prize, Stanford 2032 grand unification completed, Nobel prize, anomalies in original data set indicating an unknown boson, confirmed unknown quantum particle, Nobel prize, chromodynamics realization of bounded spiriton quantum particles, Nobel prize, detection machines invented detecting minds and ghosts, quantum particles are named the spiriton, 2036 sublime grand unification, Nobel prize, global revival 2038, global very large array first cosmic detection, Keck Hawaii, SALT Africa, God particle detection satellite launched 2040, God detection and revelations, and ending in the apocalyptic revelation of the final judgment days where the universe is transformed into a new dimension as believers souls join Yahweh, Jesus and Allah in the quantum domain, and the condemned are destroyed in catastrophic earthquakes, floods, and nuclear exchanges triggered by the Antichrist, the ending.

I was born Michael Derrick Reid. My mother had my legal name changed to Derrick Michael Reid when I was two years old. Apparently, God wanted Michael to drill for truths for a half-century before wielding a righteous sword. God's plan is amazing as now I carry Archangel Michael's righteous sword for Jesus, Yahweh and Allah in my heart, a driller for truths and a defender of the faith. Archangel Michael is a prominent figure in Judaism, Christianity, and Islam, often depicted as a warrior angel, champion of justice, and protector of God's people. He is considered a powerful being who fights evil and guides humanity, often invoked for protection and divine intervention.

Archangel Michael has key theological aspects. Warrior and Defender: He is frequently portrayed as a warrior, armed with a sword, and depicted in combat with or triumphing over evil forces like Satan or the dragon. Champion of Justice: Michael is associated with divine justice and is believed to fight for the reestablishment of righteousness. Protector of God's People: He is considered the guardian of Israel and the protector of God's chosen people. Guidance and Intervention: Michael is believed to communicate with humans, offering guidance and protection. Significance in Religious Texts: He is mentioned by name in the Torah (Judaism), the Bible (Christianity), and the Quran (Islam). Artistic Depictions: Michael is often depicted in art with a sword, shield, and other symbols of his warrior role, as well as in scenes of combat or triumph over evil. Feast Days: He is celebrated on various dates depending on the religious tradition, such as September 29 in the Western Church and November 8 in the Eastern Orthodox Church. Invocation: People often invoke Michael for protection from evil, guidance, and courage. Patron Saint: He is considered the patron saint of soldiers, police officers, firefighters, and sailors, among others. Angel of Death: In some Christian traditions, Michael is also seen as the angel of death, guiding souls to the afterlife.

I seek to unify the three Abrahamic religions, Christianity, Judaism, and Islam, in brotherly love for restoring domestic tranquility and ending wars, with Jesus, Yahweh, and Allah blessing us all worldwide, including 2.38 billion Christians, 15.7 million Jews, and 1.9 billion Muslims, all joining hands worldwide in brotherly love, mutual respect and harmony. Humans are imperfect and have misinterpreted spiritual messages and scripture. It is possible Jesus, Yahweh and Allah are one in the same in superposition in a cosmic quantum singularity, that God the Father is Yahweh, God the Son is Jesus, and God the Spirit is Allah, just maybe.

The divine mystery is pervasive for allowing free will. Blessed are those who believe but have not seen God's heavenly and earthly revelations. Condemned are those who have seen but will not believe.

I feel the Prince of Peace has commissioned me to unite the three Abrahamic Religions in brotherly love, mutual respect, and harmony. I feel God has commissioned me to restore the financial health and founding principles of the country. I know how to accomplish these desired results. I will not shrink from these callings with the Almighty in my heart. I call upon all Christians, Jews, and Muslims to stand shoulder to shoulder in brotherly love, mutual respect and harmony as an American beacon to the world for world peace. Jesus, Yahweh and Allah will smile upon the world. I have devised a way to bring the three Abrahamic religions together in brotherly love on a global scale. This is how we end the wars and defeat evil, not through guns and divisiveness, but through mutual respect and love. God's grace is unbounded and may now be actuated for the good of mankind. God's Will will be done.

Archangel Michael

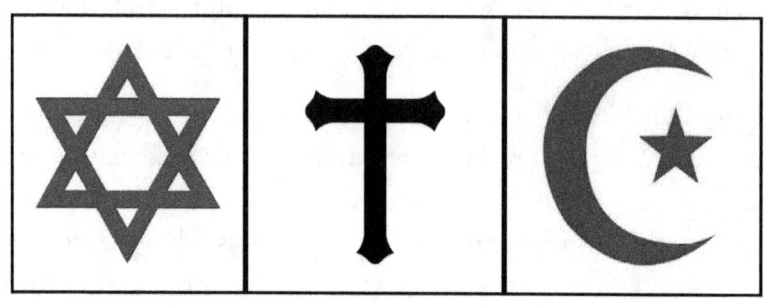

Judaism   Christianity   Islam

Praise the Supreme Ruler of the Universe!

Onward Christian Soldier

I beseech your prayers, support and blessings.

Instructional Appendix

Part I, Theology, Divine Creation and Intervention

Part II, Physics, Quantum Particles and Cosmology

Part III, Genetics, DNA Sequencing and Evolution

Part IV, Consciousness, Creative Mind and Thought

Part I, Theology

In the Beginning, there was the Word, and the Word is immaterial, spaceless, timeless, all-powerful, all-knowing, personal, and good, the alpha and the omega, the eternal, uncaused cause, God Almighty.

Without a Judgment Day, There is No Justice.

Theistic Creed

https://youtube.com/watch?v=0lRkEYoBH8U

Genesis

https://youtube.com/watch?v=aFMLEhaJx9Y

Spirit in the Sky

https://youtube.com/watch?v=swIcX57vYDI

God and Science Part I

https://youtube.com/watch?v=DoLTcv-RPdM

God and Science Part II

https://youtube.com/watch?v=dLQGr0Zmq7c

Heaven is a Place on Earth

https://youtube.com/watch?v=05V4CgSL0lw

Intelligent Design

https://youtube.com/watch?v=vl802lHAk5Y

The God Hypothesis

https://youtube.com/watch?v=z_8PPO-cAlA

Proof of God

https://youtube.com/watch?v=KbbE8ZLzcRk

Amazing Grace

https://youtube.com/watch?v=u4qbmPpfG6s

Physics of God

https://youtube.com/watch?v=v3nHavT4Fyk

Divine Cosmological Fine Tuning

https://youtube.com/watch?v=dwa6LfZlGN8

Divine Aspects of Reality

https://youtube.com/watch?v=f0QPWQR5f9Q

Something rather than Nothing

https://youtube.com/watch?v=cfmewf2DoKU

God's Mercy and Power are Infinite and Good

Part II, Physics

Big Bang Creation, Quantum Grand Unification, Space-Time, Quantum Particles, Nucleons, Atoms, Molecules, to Matter, the faith in Physics to be everywhere the same is a faith in the certainty of a ubiquitous mathematical order, a mathematical description of how matter and space-time work, a modeling of God's Works.

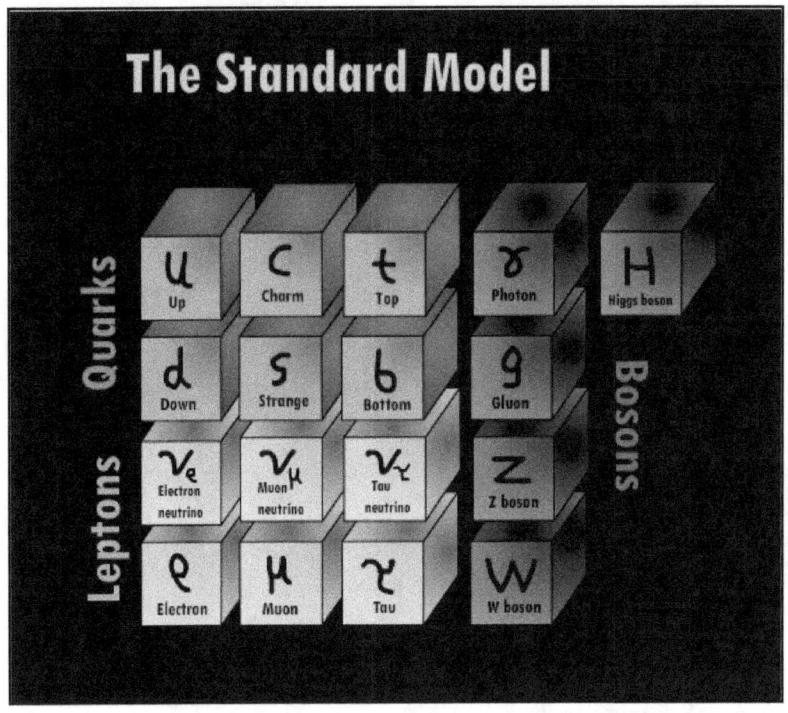

The Standard Model of Particle Physics

Physics World Knowledge

https://youtube.com/watch?v=gKrjOD3ZeO0

Atomic Bohr Model

https://youtube.com/watch?v=_Gt7mo8SNkA

Chemical Elements

https://youtube.com/watch?v=ZJQjjBR6PbY

Maxwells Equations

https://youtube.com/watch?v=SS4tcajTsW8

Electromagnetism

https://youtube.com/watch?v=dOusl55nTZk

Electrostatic Forces

https://youtube.com/watch?v=NK-BxowMIfg

Atomic Illusion of Quantum Reality

https://youtube.com/watch?v=KFS4oiVDeBI

Wave-Particle Duality

https://youtube.com/watch?v=k581_XpaTnU

Planck Constants

https://youtube.com/watch?v=5kuRatz2rj0

General Relativity

https://youtube.com/watch?v=DYq774z4dws

Special Relativity

https://youtube.com/watch?v=uTyAI1LbdgA

Standard Model of Quantum Particles

https://youtube.com/watch?v=mYcLuWHzfmE

Quantum Particles

https://youtube.com/watch?v=QPAxzr6ihu8

Quantum Mechanics

https://youtube.com/watch?v=LqY3TUW7skI

Quantum Mechanics Time Arrow

https://youtube.com/watch?v=wXJ9eQ7qTQk

Quantum Mechanics Erasure Experiment

https://youtube.com/watch?v=H6HLjpj4Nt4

Higgs Bozon and Higgs Field at Spin Zero

https://youtube.com/watch?v=kixAljyfdqU

Quantum Fields Feynman Diagrams

https://youtube.com/watch?v=fG52mXN-uWI

Relativistic Universal Symmetries

https://youtube.com/watch?v=hF_uHfSoOGA

Quantum Fields

https://youtube.com/watch?v=zNVQfWC_evg

Quantum Field Theory

https://youtube.com/watch?v=MmG2ah5Df4g

Quantum Electrodynamics part I

https://youtube.com/watch?v=X-FEU4mQWtE

Quantum Electrodynamics part II

https://youtube.com/watch?v=PutOOpAkjQ4

Quantum Electrodynamics Cassiopeia

https://youtube.com/watch?v=KZ67q4pv0HI

Quantum Chromodynamics

https://youtube.com/watch?v=FoR3hq5b5yE

Heisenberg Uncertainty Principle

https://youtube.com/watch?v=uZDhCW-PTRM

Quantum Foam

https://youtube.com/watch?v=J3xLuZNKhlY

Quantum Theory of Everything

https://youtube.com/watch?v=_izocEgArtQ

Quantum Gravity

https://youtube.com/watch?v=YNEBhwimJWs

Undetected Gravitons

https://youtube.com/watch?v=nQjzZjYfzjg

Physical Quantum Grand Unification

https://youtube.com/watch?v=gKrjOD3ZeO0

Big Bang Grand Unification

https://youtube.com/watch?v=uBk-Wst_7aA

Inflationary Cosmology

https://youtube.com/watch?v=5JM9RJFMHgc

Big Bang Cosmology

https://youtube.com/watch?v=Y5rZ58Q_0zk

Cosmic Microwave Background Radiation

https://youtube.com/watch?v=P_deJsiCNSk

Dark Matter and Rotating Galaxies

https://youtube.com/watch?v=o79szJBtQ5E

Dark Energy and Cosmic Expansion

https://youtube.com/watch?v=fnkj6fD_i9o

Origin of Matter and Time

https://youtube.com/watch?v=fHRqibyNMpw

Matter and Mass

https://youtube.com/watch?v=gSKzgpt4HBU

Mass and Energy

https://youtube.com/watch?v=HfHjzomqbZc

Holographic Universe

https://youtube.com/watch?v=HIJ44AtCCi8

The Big Bang Definitely Happened

https://youtube.com/watch?v=aPStj2ZuXug

The Mathematical Universe

https://youtube.com/watch?v=_3UxvycpqYo

Gravitational Waves

https://youtube.com/watch?v=Ak6Dh3RyIk8

Quantum Physics Disproves Materialism

https://youtube.com/watch?v=wM0IKLv7KrE

What Everything Really Is

https://youtube.com/watch?v=euNr9PozCmg

Matter Enabling Electron Spin

https://youtube.com/watch?v=EK_6OzZAh5k

Mankind's Place in the Universe

https://youtube.com/watch?v=6eAMGN69B5k

Spin ½ Quantum Particles

https://youtube.com/watch?v=ACZC_XEyg9U

Anthropic Principle

https://youtube.com/watch?v=NMV9t-3rFNs

How the Universe Began

https://youtu.be/3Illx0WkCxU?si=1EDfpkxhA68xclt5

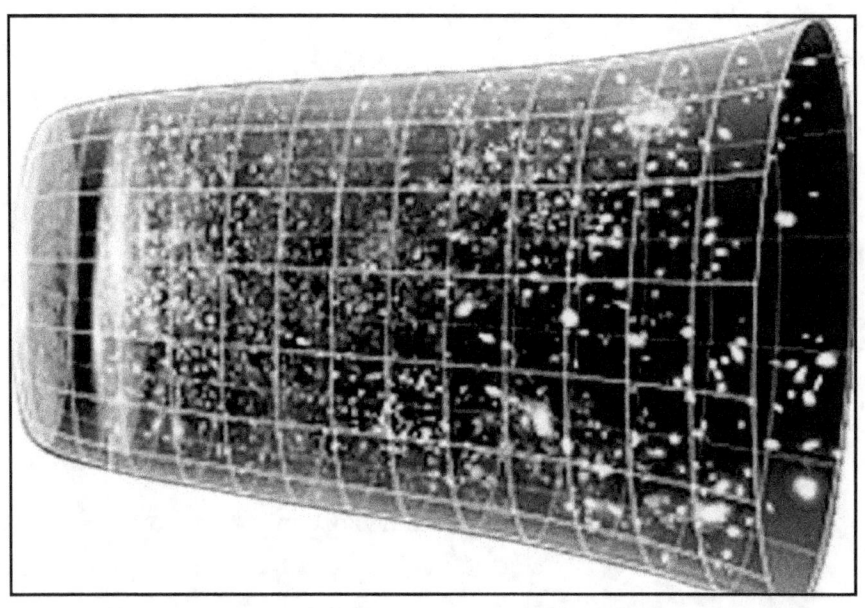

Big Bang Expansion of the known Universe

Part III, Genetics

The impossibility of DNA spontaneously randomly originating from a chemical primordial soup and the degradation of morphologies through random mutations preventing the evolution of species renders intelligent design as the only plausible explanation for life-originating existence and evolving biological adaptations and morphologies, and intelligent design requires a creative conscious mind.

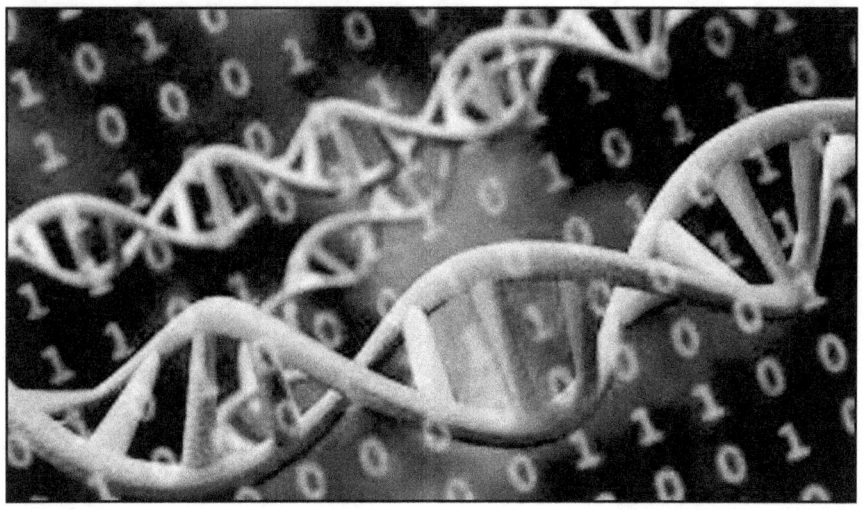

Life-enabling DNA is Code Created by Design

Origin of Life

https://youtube.com/watch?v=zU7Lww-sBPg

Random Mutations Degrade Biology

https://youtube.com/watch?v=aA-FcnLsF1g

Cambrian Explosion

https://youtube.com/watch?v=wLpSb-iDNyw

Signature in the Cell

https://youtube.com/watch?v=eW6egHV6jAw

Human Migration Genetic Markers

https://youtube.com/watch?v=dhOYxbsifkI

Irreducible Complexity

https://youtube.com/watch?v=yudmK5jZy9A

Improbable Darwinism

https://youtube.com/watch?v=noj4phMT9OE

Impossible Darwinism

https://youtube.com/watch?v=8FYZl8fc_PQ

Evolutionary Biological Tree

https://youtube.com/watch?v=aXKAMR94-rc

Neanderthals and Denisovans

https://youtube.com/watch?v=54zB8FOlFcE

Evolution Secrets

https://youtube.com/watch?v=BJm5jHhJNBI

Genetic Journey of Man

https://youtube.com/watch?v=W_xTG6VXlIQ

Fossil Record

https://youtube.com/watch?v=V15sjy7gtVM

Intelligent Design

https://youtube.com/watch?v=vl802lHAk5Y

DNA Code rewriting by Mind created Speciation.

Part IV Consciousness

The physical order, God's Works, is and can only possibly be derived from the mind, God's Word, where the Conscious Mind is primary and Matter is derivative, the mind being the source of all creativity and creation, and when the mind is infinite, all works are then possible.

The Thinker, I think, therefore I am.

Consciousness is Primary to Reality

https://youtube.com/watch?v=dYjnZCy_ZK4

Universal Conscious Life

https://youtube.com/watch?v=oFZFbFD8uk0

Baffling Consciousness

https://youtube.com/watch?v=hTIk9MN3T6w

Illusory Consciousness

https://youtube.com/watch?v=2aPmC_zQ8bI

Consciousness

https://youtube.com/watch?v=uhRhtFFhNzQ

Secrets of Consciousness

https://youtube.com/watch?v=Tgc_jvnuyqs

Consciousness Hard Problem

https://youtube.com/watch?v=LW59lMvxmY4

Consciousness Hard Problem II

https://youtube.com/watch?v=Myl_gnRxh94

Consciousness Brain Physics

https://youtube.com/watch?v=xGbgDf4HCHU

Panpsychism

https://youtube.com/watch?v=ejGn6eQsVf8

Brain Micro-tubials

https://youtube.com/watch?v=43vuOpJY46s

Dualism Explanation of Consciousness

https://youtube.com/watch?v=aUfOCY6cg4E

Brain Consciousness

https://youtube.com/watch?v=LyPEgKuqrtM

Consciousness Meta Problem

https://youtube.com/watch?v=OsYUWtLQBS0

Consciousness is an Illusion

https://youtube.com/watch?v=2aPmC_zQ8bI

Consciousness Neuroscience

https://youtube.com/watch?v=k_ZTNmkIiBc

Intelligent Consciousness

https://youtube.com/watch?v=HhU8wvmHmUY

The Infinite Mind

https://youtube.com/watch?v=Az18Onc0e58

Conscious Agents

https://youtube.com/watch?v=SL8wopYLM7Y

Quantum Theory of Consciousness

https://youtube.com/watch?v=L8OrNUzbmS8

Quantum Consciousness

https://youtube.com/watch?v=bqk1oL42r5s

Quantum Conscious Soul

https://youtube.com/watch?v=K1qx_jgFZhc

Unification of Physics Consciousness and God

https://youtube.com/watch?v=v3nHavT4Fyk

The Source of Consciousness

https://youtube.com/watch?v=CmuYrnOVmfk

Brain Physics of Consciousness

https://youtube.com/watch?v=xGbgDf4HCHU

The Physics of Consciousness

https://youtube.com/watch?v=h_VeDKVG7e0

Noncomputational Consciousness

https://youtube.com/watch?v=hXgqik6HXc0

Quantum Consciousness

https://youtube.com/watch?v=axGqpYKDsDw

Quantum Physics of Consciousness

https://youtube.com/watch?v=gfmcEbD64XY

Afterlife by Albert Einstein

https://youtu.be/hn0mhRZ-dk8

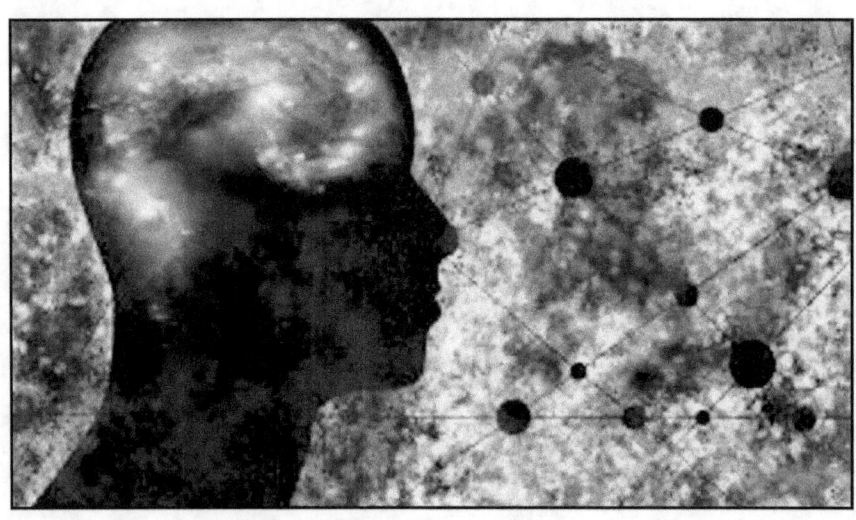

The Conscious Mind is The Source of Creativity.

THE END

EPILOGUE

My fellow countrymen, did you notice US Debt was downgraded in May 2025, after the national debt limit was raised by 5T$? The fuse has been lit, as bond prices fall, as interest rates rise, that it may eventually trigger a national collapse in uncontrollable positive feedback. I will monitor the possible pending collapse in real time at DMRCommentary. com. There is a way to prevent doom and catastrophe, but that will take courage from the voting public. I trust God will save our beloved country.

A Derrick Michael Reid 2028 Presidency is now indispensable. As of January 17, 2025, the national debt of the United States was $36.2 trillion, expecting to increase 5T$ further still over the next few years. The 2023 national GDP was 27.7T$. The debt to GDP ratio is 36.2/27.7 which is equals is 1.30. The collapse threshold is historically 1.25. The point of no return has been breached. Economic, monetary and societal collapse and implosion are now inevitable based on 600+ imploded prior fiat regimes. The national debt and inflation are obviously unsustainable.

Some hope that DOGE (Department of Government Efficiency) is the solution. Efficiency will fail, because efficiency is not the problem. Debt is the problem. Russia and China have already passed the fiat collapse threshold and are currently imploding. The US has just recently passed the fiat collapse threshold. Diplomatic, monetary hegemony and military strength may delay the inevitable a bit longer, but societal complex collapse is on its way to the good ole USA. To prevent the inevitable societal complex collapse, in the USA, there is only one solution, implementing the American Freedom Platform. Not only will the American Freedom Platform significantly increase our liberties and freedoms from government, and restore the US financial health, it will also prevent a USA societal complex implosion and resulting national catastrophe.

American Freedom Platform: Eliminate state and federal income taxes; Eliminate capital gains, gift, and probate taxes; Eliminate individual state and federal tax filings; Eliminate business state tax filings; Eliminate individual IRS tax audits; Eliminate state and federal deficits; Eliminate state debts and national debt; Eliminate monetary inflation and deflation; Eliminate Federal Reserve Notes and the FED; Eliminate hot wars and entanglements; Eliminate political and civil divisiveness; Eliminate Abrahamic and cultural divisiveness; Transfer SBA loans to the states; Transfer federal welfare complex to the states; Transfer federal student loans to the states; Create the Bank of the United States and USD; Create SBA grants for start up enterprises; Create DEd research grants and scholarships; Create national business sales-revenue flat tax; Create national business IRS flat tax filings; and Create a political coalition US government.

American Freedom Coalition including: Democrats; Republicans; Libertarians; Independents; and Greens, comprising: Blue-Dog Democrats; Traditional Liberal Democrats; Progressive Democrats (renouncing Federal Socialism); MAGA Republicans; America First Republicans; Traditional Conservative Republicans; Rhino Republicans (renouncing Federal Socialism); Moderate Libertarians; Minarchist Libertarians (renouncing Federal Anarchy); Anti-Corruption Independents; Americana Independents; Environmental Greens; Wall Street Occupiers; Tax Tea Partiers and Tax Protesters; Government Corruption and Waste Watchdogs; US Citizens supporting Traditional Americana; and US Citizens supporting Liberty, Freedom, Peace and Prosperity, For Capturing 2/3 of the Popular Vote.